A Basket Full of White Eggs

Riddle-Poems by Brian Swann

Pictures by PONDER GOEMBEL

ORCHARD BOOKS • NEW YORK • LONDON
A division of Franklin Watts, Inc.

With special thanks to Sandy Hardy
— B.S.

Orchard Books, 387 Park Avenue South, New York, New York 10016
Orchard Books Great Britain, 10 Golden Square, London W1R 3AF England
Orchard Books Australia, 14 Mars Road, Lane Cove, New South Wales 2066
Orchard Books Canada, 20 Torbay Road, Markham, Ontario 23P 1G6

Orchard Books is a division of Franklin Watts, Inc.

Manufactured in the United States of America.
Book design by Mina Greenstein
The text of this book is set in Barcelona Book.
The illustrations are watercolor and colored pencil, reproduced in halftone.
1   3   5   7   9   10   8   6   4   2

Library of Congress Cataloging-in-Publication Data
Swann, Brian. A basket full of white eggs.
Summary: Proverbs from many countries, including Italy, Saudi Arabia, and
the Philippines.   1. Proverbs.   (1. Proverbs)   I. Goembel, Ponder, ill.
II. Title.   PN6405.S93   1988   398′.9′21   87-11220
ISBN 0-531-05734-8   ISBN 0-531-08334-9 (lib. bdg.)

Riddles ask
to be answered * To
the question "What am
I?" a single word or simple
phrase is usually the solution,
and often answers are easier
than you might think at first *
Guessing them is the fun! *
The answers to the riddles
that follow are revealed in the
paintings * But you may check
yourself by turning to the last
page of the book, where the answers are revealed in words *

4

Over a flat rock
a tomato's redness
slowly spreads out.
—*Mayan*

A lady comes, clad
in a hundred dresses.

When the wind blows
we see
many eyes under the dresses.
—*Lithuanian*

We enter by three doors.
We exit by one.
—Aztec

Someone went out at night
and lost her silver buckle.
The moon found it,
but only the sun
caught it.
—*Lithuanian*

I dove into the lake, and
under the water
looked back up.

The water I'd jumped in
was now
hard ice.
—*North Pontic Turkic*

We are riding
upstream in our
red canoes.
—*Ten'a (Alaska)*

I go through the valley
slapping my palms together
like the women in town
who are making tortillas.
—*Aztec*

O tree in the forest—
no roots, no leaves—
so full of fine branches!
—*Visayan (Philippines)*

The child is walking.
Its mother is crawling.
—*Yoruba (Nigeria)*

20

I run, I run.
When I arrive
I bend down and
let fall
all my white hairs.
—Visayan (Philippines)

Far off in the distance,
something white is
chasing a flash
of red fire.

—*Ten'a (Alaska)*

In the sea a branch,
on the branch a nest,
in the nest a dove.
When she sings the whole world trembles.
—*Italian*

It's black and trickles down,
trickles down from the hill:
sweeter than sugar,
more delicious than honey.

—*Riyadh Arabic (Saudi Arabia)*

28

You cannot shake the dust
from the lynx's coat,
nor pick the pearls
from the distant sea.

My grandfather's blue silk
tunic's so long it cannot
be folded. It is studded
with coins. They
cannot be counted.

—North Pontic Turkic

ANSWERS

Jacket	Stars	16–17	Butterfly
		18–19	Deer
4–5	Sunrise	20–21	Squash
6–7	Hen and chicks	22–23	Wave
8–9	Shirt	24–25	Fox's tail
10–11	Dew	26–27	Thunder
12–13	Mirror	28–29	Sleep
14–15	Salmon	30–31	Night sky

* * * * *

POET'S NOTE

The riddles in this book are new poems drawn from the following sources: Jacket and pages 26–27: Carlo Lapucci, ed. *Indovinelle italiani*, Firenze (1977); pages 4–5: Margaret Park Redfield, "The Folk Literature of a Yucatecan Town," *Carnegie Institution: Contributions to American Archaeology*, Vol. III, Nos. 13–19 (1937); pages 6–7 and 10–11: Jonas Balys, "Forty Lithuanian Riddles," *Journal of American Folklore*, Vol. 36 (1924); pages 8–9 and 16–17: Bernadino de Sahagún, *Historia general de las cosas de Nueva España*. Mexico City (1956); pages 14–15 and 24–25: Fr. Julius Jette, "Riddles of the Ten'a Indians," *Anthropos VIII* (1913); pages 12–13 and 30–31: Andreas Tietze, *The Koman Riddles and Turkic Folklore* (a collection of riddles from Codex Cumanicus, a 14th century document), University of California Press (1966); pages 18–19 and 22–23: Maria Luz C. Vilches, *Visayan Riddles*, Divine Word University Publications, Tacloban City, Philippines (1978); pages 20–21: William R. Bascom, "Literary Style in Yoruba Riddles," *Journal of American Folklore*, Vol. 62 (1949); pages 28–29: Charles Thomas Scott, "A Linguistic Study of Persian and Arabic Riddles: A Language-Centered Approach to Genre Definition," The Universiy of Texas, Ph.D. (1963).